RADIANT YOU

Affirmations for Tween & Teen Girls

Published by Bardolf & Company

RADIANT YOU
Affirmations for Teen & Tween Girls

ISBN 978-1-938842-64-1

Copyright © 2023 by Dawne Christine

All rights reserved. No part of this book may be used or reproduced in any form or by any electronic or mechanical means, including information storage and retrieval systems, without permission in writing from the publisher.

For information write:

Bardolf & Company
www.bardolfandcompany.com
941-232-0113

Cover Image: *Matthew James Carmoega*

Dedication

For my beautiful daughter Ryleigh
and all the girls who have faced challenges
with confidence, self-esteem, and self-love.
You are not alone on this journey.

I want you to know that you are more than enough.
You are beautiful just as you are, and no one has the
right to make you feel otherwise.
Don't allow others to diminish your worth
or make you feel less
than the amazing person you are.

Don't be afraid to stand out and express yourself.
Speak up when you have something to say.
Let your light shine brightly.
Follow your dreams and listen to your heart.
Have the confidence to know that you can
achieve anything you set your mind to.

Don't let anybody extinguish the light
that burns within you.
Remember that if you can think it,
you can create it.

An affirmation opens the door.
It's a beginning point
on the path to change.

> —Louise L. Hay
> motivational speaker and author

It's the repetition of affirmation
that leads to belief,
and once that belief
becomes a deep conviction,
things begin to happen.

> —Claude M. Bristol
> lawyer, lecturer, writer

RADIANT YOU

Affirmations for Tween & Teen Girls

Dawne Christine, CLC, CHC

Bardolf & Company
Sarasota, Florida

Contents

Introduction	7
What Are Affirmations?	8
How Affirmations Helped Me	9
How Affirmations Work	11
How to Use Affirmations	13
Chapter 1: Building Confidence	17
Chapter 2: Being Your Authentic Self	21
Chapter 3: Fitting In	25
Chapter 4: Shifting Negative Thoughts	29
Chapter 5: Facing Bullies with Courage	31
Chapter 6: True Beauty	35
Chapter 7: Finding Yourself	37
Chapter 8: Hormones & Emotions	41
Additional Advice	45
Afterword	47
Acknowledgments	49

Introduction

Prepare for a life-changing journey of self-discovery and empowerment! Self-realization is an adventure, unlocking the mysteries of your true being.

This book is your guiding light in a world that pressures you to conform. It will let you explore the heart of confidence, the belief in your abilities and self-worth, and the ability to nurture the superpower of self-belief and resilience. You can learn to rise above the crowd, attract genuine friends, and stand tall against bullies.

So, let's navigate the roller coaster of your teenage years with wisdom and self-care. It's time to unleash your authentic self and let your radiance shine. Your extraordinary journey begins now!

What Are Affirmations?

Affirmations are powerful statements to say to yourself so that you combat worries, and feel better and more confident. They are like little pep talks you give yourself to feel happier and more positive. They're encouraging words or phrases that you repeat to yourself to make you believe in yourself and feel stronger.

For example, you might say, "I am strong and capable," "I can do anything I set my mind to," or "I am a kind and awesome person." These statements can boost your mood and make you feel more confident. Affirmations are like your personal cheerleaders, helping you feel great about yourself and your abilities.

They're like a superpower for your self-esteem! Affirmations have the power to shape thoughts and beliefs. They don't magically make problems disappear, but they'll equip you with the mindset and confidence needed to overcome obstacles and achieve your goals. It's like having a secret weapon that will empower you to be the best version of yourself.

How Affirmations Helped Me

Let me share a personal experience of how affirmations have made a profound impact on my life. I didn't have a very supportive environment from my family growing up. My mother had a way of using hurtful words to undermine my self-esteem and confidence that seemed to pierce right through me. Those words took a heavy toll on my self-worth, and over time, I started to believe that I wasn't worthy of much.

Carrying these negative beliefs into my adult years had a profound impact on my life. I found myself plagued by self-doubt. It was as if those hurtful words from my past had become a permanent soundtrack in my mind, holding me back from pursuing my dreams and believing in my own abilities.

It wasn't until I stumbled upon the concept of affirmations that things began to change. Learning about how affirmations could help reprogram those negative thoughts was a turning point for me. I started to use positive affirmations daily, repeating phrases like, "I am worthy," "I believe in myself," and "I deserve happiness."

At first, it felt strange and uncomfortable, like I was trying to convince myself of something I didn't fully believe. But as I persisted, the affirmations slowly started to replace the hurtful words and beliefs that had held me back for so long. It was like planting seeds of self-love and watching them grow.

Gradually, I began to rebuild my self-esteem and regain my confidence. I realized that I was indeed worthy of love, success, and happiness. Affirmations became a lifeline, helping me challenge and replace the negative beliefs that had haunted me for years. Over time, those affirmations started to seep into my subconscious mind. I began to genuinely believe in my capabilities.

Affirmations have become part of my daily routine. I use them to boost my self-esteem, tackle challenges, and maintain a positive outlook.

My journey is a testament to the transformative power of affirmations. They not only helped me break free from the chains of a painful past but also empowered me to embrace a brighter, more confident future. Today, I stand tall, knowing that I deserve all the good things life has to offer.

How Affirmations Work

Affirmations have a remarkable impact on your brain and consciousness. Here's how they work and what they do:

Affirmations serve as a tool to rewire your brain for positivity. When you repeat positive statements regularly, your brain starts to create new neural pathways that reinforce these positive beliefs. This process helps weaken the existing negative thought patterns and replaces them with more constructive ones.

Affirmations boost your self-esteem by promoting positive self-talk. Instead of focusing on self-criticism or doubt, affirmations encourage self-encouragement and self-belief. This shift in mindset can lead to increased self-esteem and self-worth.

Positive affirmations can reduce stress and anxiety levels. When you repeat calming and reassuring affirmations, your brain responds by releasing neurochemicals that counteract stress hormones, helping you feel more relaxed and in control.

Affirmations can improve your focus and clarity of thought. By affirming your abilities and goals, you provide your brain with a clear target. This can help you concentrate on what you want to achieve and filter out distractions.

Affirmations can make you more resilient in the face of challenges. When you repeat affirmations related to your ability to overcome obstacles, your brain internalizes the idea that you have the strength and capability to navigate difficulties.

Affirmations can be powerful motivators. When you affirm your goals and your determination to achieve them, your brain responds by releasing dopamine, a neurotransmitter associated with motivation and reward. This can increase your drive to work toward your aspirations.

Positive affirmations can enhance your overall mood. By focusing on uplifting statements, you encourage your brain to produce "feel-good" neurotransmitters like serotonin and endorphins, which can elevate your mood and create a sense of happiness.

Affirmations can reshape your self-image. When you repeatedly tell yourself positive things about who you are and what you're capable of, your brain begins to accept these statements as facts, leading to a more positive self-image.

How To Use Affirmations

Create an Affirmation notebook for yourself. Start by finding a special notebook or journal that appeals to you. You can decorate it with colors and stickers to make it your own. This will be your special place for affirmations.

To choose Affirmations, you can find them in books, online, or make up your own. They should be about things you want or how you want to feel. For example, "I am confident," "I am kind," or "I am strong."

Find a quiet and comfy spot. It could be your bedroom, a cozy corner, or even out-of-doors on a patio, in the backyard, in a park or other natural setting outside in nature. It should be a place where you can feel relaxed.

Before you start, take a few deep breaths. Inhale through your nose, hold for a moment, and exhale through your mouth. This helps you relax and focus.

Now, say your affirmations out loud. Say them with confidence and believe in what you're saying.

Why is it important to say affirmations out loud?

It makes them more powerful: When you say affirmations out loud, you hear them from the outside through your ears, and your brain pays extra attention.

It helps you remember: Hearing words that way is also a great way to remember them. So, when you say affirmations out loud, you're more likely to remember them throughout the day.

As you say the affirmations, imagine these words becoming true for you. As you say the affirmations, try to picture in your mind what it would be like if they came true. Visualize yourself being confident, kind, or whatever your affirmation says.

Make this a daily routine. You can do it in the morning to start your day, at lunch or during a break, or before going to bed to end the day on a good note.

Be patient and say your affirmations every day. Just like planting seeds, it takes time for affirmations to grow and work. It takes the brain 29 days to build a new habit.

Note changes. As you keep using your affirmation book, pay attention to how you feel and write down when you start feeling more confident, positive, and happier.

**Success is not final; failure is not fatal:
It is the courage to act that counts.**
— Winston Churchill
British statesman and writer

It is confidence in our bodies, minds, and spirits that allows us to keep looking for new adventures.

— Oprah Winfrey
talk show host and producer

I taught myself confidence. When I'd walk into a room and feel scared to death, I'd tell myself, "I'm not afraid of anybody." And people believed me.

—Priyanka Chopra Jonas
actress and producer

With confidence, you have won before you have started.

—Marcus Garvey
activist and orator

Chapter 1

Building Confidence

Confidence is a feeling of self-assurance and belief in your own abilities, judgment, and worth. It's the belief that you can handle situations, overcome challenges, and achieve your goals. Confidence is an inner strength that helps you face life's ups and downs with courage and optimism. When you're confident, you trust yourself and your decisions. You're not easily shaken by setbacks or criticism, and you have a positive self-image.

Confidence isn't about being perfect, or knowing everything ahead of time, or never experiencing doubt; it's about moving forward despite obstacles and trusting yourself to handle whatever comes your way.. Confidence is a feeling of self-assurance and belief in yourself. It's like having a trusted friend inside your mind who reminds you that you've got what it takes.

Imagine you're embarking on an exciting adventure, like climbing a mountain or performing on a stage. Confidence is that inner voice that says, "I can do this!" even when you're faced with challenges or self-doubt. It's the courage to step out of your comfort zone, try new things, and trust in your abilities.

Confidence isn't something you're born with; it's a skill you can develop over time, like learning to ride a bike. It grows when you set goals, face your fears, and celebrate your successes. And here's the magical part: the more you believe in yourself, the more incredible things you can achieve. So, trust yourself, be kind to yourself, and let yourself shine!

I AM CONFIDENT, AND IT'S MY BEST OUTFIT; I ROCK IT DAILY.

I am starting with self-acceptance because confidence begins within.

I am inhaling confidence, and with each exhale, doubt disappears.

I am beautiful, and I wear confidence daily.

I am silent in my confidence; insecurities have no voice.

I am radiating confidence because it's magnetic.

I am a believer in my power to create change.

I AM CONFIDENT, AND IT'S MY BEST MAKEUP.

I am empowered by my secret weapon, which is my confidence.

I am cultivating confidence through self-acceptance.

I am on the path to success because I have confidence.

I am building my success on the foundation of confidence.

I AM CREATING MAGIC BY BELIEVING IN MY CONFIDENCE.

I am a superhero; my superpower is confidence.

I am sparking success because I have confidence.

I am taking the first step towards success with my confidence.

Always be a first-rate version of yourself and not a second-rate version of someone else.

> — Judy Garland
> American actress and singer

To be successful, you must be so unique, you must be so different that if people want what you have, they have to come to you to get it.

> —Walt Disney
> animator, film producer, and entrepreneur

Authenticity is the daily practice of letting go who we think we are supposed to be and embracing who we are.

> —Brené Brown
> American professor, author and podcast host

Chapter 2

Being Your Authentic Self

Whether your passionate about clothes, math, painting, dancing, or sharing jokes, there's no need to hide it! Being true to yourself means allowing your inner radiance to shine brightly. Embracing your authentic self is similar to proudly displaying yourself as a unicorn for all to see, announcing, 'This is me!'

People are as diverse as trees in a vast, enchanting forest—some tower tall, others stand lower to the ground; some have leaves, others have needles; still others have berries, acorns, or chestnuts. Each possesses its unique charm. It's the diversity that enhances the forest's breathtaking beauty! So embrace your uniqueness. Don't conceal your special talents, or anything that defines the wonderful you.

Your mission is to embark on a journey of self-discovery. What brings you joy? What activities fill you with happiness? The trek will uncover concealed paths leading straight to your heart and mind. Along the way, you'll become acquainted with the remarkable person you are becoming. The thrilling part involves engaging in activities you adore, even if they differ from your friends' interests. Your expedition of self-discovery is the most exhilarating adventure of all.

So, take pride in your quirks, and don't shy away from standing out. Be the special tree. Be the unicorn. Be the rare, shimmering gem in the treasure chest of the world. Remain true to yourself, embrace your distinctive qualities, and revel in exploring all the marvelous aspects that define the Radiant You!"

**I am embracing my uniqueness;
it's my superpower.**

**I am the one who defines my beauty;
I won't let others do it for me.**

I am never afraid to stand out.

I AM CONFIDENT BECAUSE I AM AUTHENTIC.

I am empowered because I believe in myself.

**I am owning my truth;
that's where my empowerment begins.**

I am different, and that's my superpower.

I am authentic and empowered in my true self.

**I am armed with confidence;
it's my secret weapon.**

I am strong because
I find strength in vulnerability.

I am embracing my individuality.

I am embracing my uniqueness with pride.

I AM EMBRACING MY INNER WARRIOR.

I am embracing my inner champion.

I am embracing my inner leader.

I am embracing my inner hero.

**I am embracing my true self
with open arms.**

I AM EMBRACING MY INNER STRENGTH.

I am embracing my inner fire.

I am embracing my unique potential.

Why fit in when you were born to stand out?

— Theodor Seuss Geisel
"Dr. Seuss"
children's author

I think the best way to deal with fitting in is to be yourself. It sounds hard, but in the end, it's much easier than pretending to be something you're not.

—Meaghan Jette Martin
American actress

Don't worry about fitting in; it's completely overrated.

—Nicola Walker
British actress

Chapter 3

Fitting In

As you're growing up, it's natural to want to fit in and be accepted by others. But sometimes, this can make you feel like you have to be someone you're not to fit in, and that can really shake your self-confidence. There is a strong desire to be a part of a group, to have friends who get you, and to feel like you belong.

Now, fitting in isn't necessarily a bad thing. Having friends and being part of a community can be incredibly rewarding. It's just that sometimes, in the quest to belong, you might start doing things you wouldn't naturally do or pretend to be someone you're not. It's like wearing a mask—a mask that hides the real you.

And that's when things get dicey. Wearing this mask can make you doubt who you truly are. You start questioning if your real self is good enough, cool enough, or interesting enough for your friends to like. Your self-confidence takes a nosedive because you're not sure if the "you" underneath that mask is worthy of love and acceptance.

But here's the beautiful twist, the real magic happens when you embrace your true self. When you allow yourself to be authentic, flaws and all, that's when you attract the kind of friends who love you for who you are, not for who you're pretending to be. And guess what? Those friendships are the ones that boost your self-confidence to the moon and back.

So, it's okay to want to fit in and be accepted, so long as you remember that the most authentic version of you is the one your real friends will cherish most. Your uniqueness is your superpower, and real friends will celebrate that with you.

I am unique and that makes me special.

I am confident in being myself.

I AM COMFORTABLE IN MY OWN SKIN.

I am proud of my individuality.

I am surrounded by people who appreciate me for who I am.

I AM MAKING FRIENDS WHO ACCEPT ME JUST AS I AM.

I am embracing my differences because they make me shine.

I am finding my place in the world, one step at a time.

I am loved and valued by those who truly know me.

I am letting my authentic self shine brightly.

I am attracting positive and like-minded people.

I am creating connections based on shared interests and values.

I am open to forming meaningful friendships.

I am part of a diverse and accepting community.

I AM COMFORTABLE EXPRESSING MY THOUGHTS AND FEELINGS.

I am contributing my unique qualities to the world.

I am learning and growing through my experiences.

I am confident that I am exactly where I'm meant to be.

I am embracing my own journey and timeline.

I am fitting in by being true to myself.

**At any given moment,
you have the power to say:
This is not how the story
is going to end.**

> — Christine Mason Miller
> author and artist

**Once you replace negative thoughts
with positive ones, you'll start
having positive results.**

> —Willie Nelson
> singer and song writer

**You don't learn to walk by following rules.
You learn by doing and falling over.**

> —Rjchard Branson
> British business magnate

Chapter 4

Shifting Negative Thoughts

We all think negative thoughts at times when we're worried, unhappy and down on ourselves. The problems occurs when they become patterns that we repeat and inflict on ourselves. Trying to identify and change them can feel like trying to unscramble that map where all the clues are jumbled up. But it's not impossible. Once you recognize the signs and know what those tricky thoughts look like, you can start turning them into happy ones!

Think of your mind like a big book with lots of stories. In your imagination some of those stories have not-so-happy endings. But you can fix that. By rewriting your mental script you become the author of your own amazing adventures. You can change stories from sad to super happy! It's all about being the boss of your thoughts and saying, "I can do this!"

Now, here's the fun part! To conquer negative thoughts, try to notice when you're feeling worried or sad. Ask yourself, "What's making me feel this way?" Once you know, you can say positive things to yourself like, "I can do hard things," or "I am kind and amazing."

Remember, you're the heroine of your own story, and you have the power to choose happy thoughts.

**When I notice negative thoughts,
I choose to replace them with positive ones.**

I am in control of my thoughts, and I choose happiness.

I have the power to change my perspective
and find happiness in every situation.

I release all negative thoughts and embrace joy.

I focus on the good things in my life and let go of negativity.

Happiness is my natural state of being, and I choose it now.

I am grateful for the present moment and find happiness in it.

I TRANSFORM NEGATIVE ENERGY INTO POSITIVE
THOUGHTS EFFORTLESSLY.

I replace fear with hope and sadness with joy.

I find beauty and happiness in the simple things in life.

I attract positivity and radiate happiness to those around me.

I am deserving of happiness, and I allow it to flow into my life.

I release all worries and embrace a sense of peace and happiness.

I choose to see the silver lining in every situation.

I am in charge of my emotional well-being,
and I choose happiness.

I surround myself with positive thoughts that bring me joy.

I let go of the past and welcome a brighter, happier future.

I am grateful for every day,
and I fill it with happiness and love.

Chapter 5

Facing Bullies with Courage

Sadly, some people can be mean, both in person and online. Spiteful words and actions can sting, and it's natural to start questioning yourself. You might wonder, "Why are they treating me this way? What did I do to deserve this?" It's like a heavy weight on your shoulders, making you doubt your worth.

I was bullied a lot growing up and some of the hurtful comments made me doubt my worth. I am here to tell you that their words don't define you!

Here's the thing: The hurtful words and actions of bullies say more about them than about you. Your tormentors often have their issues, insecurities, or pain, and unfortunately, rather than deal with them, they choose to lash out. Bullies carry around their own bundle of negativity, and try to spill it on you. But you are not their dumping ground.

Remember, your worth isn't determined by anyone else's opinion of you. You are a unique and wonderful person just as you are, and no one has the power to take that away from you.

So, while it can be tough to endure others' negativity, try not to internalize their negativity. You're stronger than you know. Hopefully you have a support system of friends, family, and mentors who see your true worth. Focus on their love and your own belief in yourself, and you'll find the strength to rise above the storm of bullying

Here are some things that I did that helped me:

Standing Tall: Remember bullies are like little rain clouds trying to dampen your spirit. Stand tall and don't let their words or actions bring you down.

Staying Calm: When bullies see that they can't ruffle your feathers, they might give up. Stay calm and keep your cool.

Sharing with a Trusty Sidekick: They can be your parents, teachers, or a school counselor. If a bully bothers you, don't keep it a secret. Tell your sidekicks what's going on so they can help.

Using Your Words: Instead of getting upset, use your words to respond. Say things like, "I don't like it when you're mean," or "I believe in myself." Your words are powerful, and that makes the some bullies' words lose their power.

Walking Away with Confidence: Sometimes, the best move is to leave. If a bully tries to pick on you, show your confidence by calmly walking away. You're in control of your actions.

Buddying Up: You can buddy up with friends. There's strength in numbers. Bullies are less likely to bother a group than a single individual.

Reporting to Your Trusted Adults: If the bullying continues, report it to your trusted adults again. They'll step in and help you handle it.

Focusing on the Positive: Surround yourself with things that make you happy, like your favorite hobbies or spending time with friends who support you. Positive vibes are a secret weapon against negativity.

Remember, you have the strength and courage to stand up to bullies and make the world a better place for yourself.

I AM TURNING EVERY SETBACK
INTO A SETUP FOR MY COMEBACK.

I am stronger than I think.

I AM BOLD, I AM BRAVE, I AM ME.

I am a source of strength, and it comes from within.

I am empowering other girls; together, we rise.

I AM A BELIEVER IN MY POWER TO INSPIRE OTHERS.

I am cherishing every moment; life is a gift to me.

I am dreaming big and working hard for my goals.

I am limitless; my potential knows no bounds.

I am capable of achieving greatness.

I AM BUILDING CHARACTER BY EMBRACING CHALLENGES.

**I am guided by my inner beauty;
it's my guiding light.**

I am fluent in the language of kindness
that everyone understands.

I am making a difference; I believe in my ability.

I am the hero of my own story.

I am empowered by my dreams; they are my superpowers.

I am becoming stronger through overcoming obstacles.

I am shining with inner beauty,
even in the darkest moments.

I am growing stronger with every challenge life brings.

I AM RADIATING POSITIVITY; IT'S MY NATURAL GLOW.

Beauty begins the moment you decide to be yourself.

—Coco Chanel
French fashion designer

I'd rather be handsome for an hour than pretty for a week.

—Tilda Swinton
British actress

The most alluring thing a woman can have is confidence.

—Beyoncé
singer-songwriter
and business woman

Chapter 6

True Beauty

We're bombarded with images of what society often considers beautiful and "perfect" in magazines, on TV, and especially on social media. These images can make you feel like you're supposed to fit into a very specific mold of beauty, which can be incredibly challenging for your self-confidence.

But those beauty standards are not real. They're often the result of editing, filters, and unrealistic enhancements. The "candid" pictures of movie stars and other famous people in the *National Enquirer* are just them without makeup! Real people don't walk around looking like airbrushed models all the time, and that's perfectly okay!

What's important to remember is that beauty comes in all shapes, sizes, colors, and forms. Every person is a unique creation a distinctive work of art, and your individuality— your quirks, freckles, scars, and imperfections—help make you beautiful.

So, the next time you find yourself comparing your appearance to those unrealistic standards, take a step back and remind yourself that you are special and beautiful yourself. Your worth isn't determined by how closely you resemble someone else's idea of beauty. Embrace your uniqueness and love yourself for who you are—that's where true confidence and beauty shine brightest.

I am a radiant beauty with a heart full of kindness.

I am inner beauty, shining brighter than any makeup could.

I am a survivor, and my scars
tell stories of strength and resilience.

I am real beauty because I am unapologetically myself.

I am beautiful because I am comfortable in my own skin.

I am the one whose smile can change the world.

I am my character, and it's my best accessory.

I am a queen who lifts others and fixes their crowns.

I AM MORE THAN A NUMBER ON A SCALE;
MY WORTH GOES BEYOND IT.

I am inner beauty that never fades.

I am wiser because of the challenges life brings.

I am a source of inner beauty,
shining even in the darkest moments.

I AM FINDING BEAUTY IN ACTS OF KINDNESS.

I am wearing kindness as my most beautiful accessory.

**I AM EMPOWERED BY MY UNIQUE QUALITIES;
THEY ARE MY GREATEST STRENGTHS.**

I am recognizing that beauty is the true measure of beauty.

I am embracing my inner beauty,
which is my true essence.

I am understanding that kindness
is the essence of true beauty.

Chapter 7

Finding Yourself

Growing up means figuring out who you are and what you stand for. Sometimes, that journey can be confusing, and you might feel unsure of yourself along the way, like you're trying to navigate a maze without a map. You might ask yourself questions like, "Who am I?" or "What do I truly believe in?" It's okay to not have all the answers right away.

During this period of your life, you're also exposed to a wide range of experiences, beliefs, and influences. You might try to fit in with various social groups, explore different interests, and test your boundaries. It's all part of the course of understanding what fits you personally.

Remember that self-discovery is a gradual process, so be patient with yourself. It's okay to not have everything figured out. In fact, many adults are still learning about themselves even in their later years. And that includes yours truly! The key is to stay open to new experiences, listen to your inner voice, and surround yourself with supportive and understanding friends and family.

Ultimately, the journey of finding yourself is a beautiful adventure. It's about uncovering your values, passions, and the unique qualities that make you who you are. As you continue to explore, you'll gain a deeper understanding of yourself and grow in self-confidence along the way. Trust the process and know that it's okay to be a work in progress.

I AM WORTHY OF LOVE, ESPECIALLY FROM MYSELF.

I am deserving of self-care, and I prioritize it in my daily life.

I am kind and compassionate toward myself, no matter the circumstances.

I am grateful for my body and all that it does for me.

I am in tune with my needs and honor them with self-care.

I am free from self-judgment and criticism.
I am comfortable setting boundaries that protect my well-being.

I am open to self-discovery and personal growth.

I AM MINDFUL OF MY THOUGHTS,
AND I REPLACE NEGATIVITY WITH SELF-LOVE.

I am a priority in my own life, and that's okay.

I am gentle with myself during times of difficulty.

I am nurturing my mind, body, and spirit through self-care practices.

I am embracing my uniqueness and celebrating my individuality.

I am releasing the need for external validation; my self-worth comes from within.

I am forgiving of my past mistakes
and focus on my present and future.

I AM EMPOWERED TO MAKE CHOICES THAT SERVE MY WELL-BEING.

I am letting go of perfectionism
and accepting myself as I am.

I am filling my cup with self-love,
so I can pour love into the world.

**I am worthy of rest and rejuvenation,
and I allow myself to take breaks.**

**I am committed to my self-care journey,
knowing it leads to a happier, healthier life.**

**Hormones get no respect.
We think of them as the elusive chemicals
that make us a bit moody,
but these magical little molecules
do so much more.**

—Susanna Cahalan
American author

**Learn to use your emotions to think,
not think with your emotions.**

—Robert Kiyosaki
American author of
Rich Dad, Poor Dad

**Feelings are much like waves.
We can't stop them from coming
but we can choose which one to surf.**

— Jonatan Mårtensson

Chapter 8

Hormones & Emotions

Your journey through your teenage years, often includes a whirlwind of changes—both inside and out. You might experience a roller-coaster of emotions, particularly when it comes to anxiety and sadness. So, let's delve a bit deeper into why these emotions are part of your life right now and why it's crucial to cope with them.

Changing Bodies and Hormones: At your age your body undergoes incredible transformations. Hormones, sneaky chemical messengers, are playing a starring role in the process. While they're essential for growth and development, they can also throw your emotions into a tizzy.

The Hormone Hustle: Imagine your hormones as instruments in an orchestra, each playing its part in a great symphony. Sometimes the sound will be beautiful and exciting. Or, it can be erratic and noisy, with unexpected mood swings and emotional ups and downs, like a thunderstorm in the middle of a sunny day.

Understanding Anxiety: Ever experience a jittery feeling in your stomach, racing thoughts, and a sense of unease? You may feel anxious about school, friendships, or the future. Guess what? You're normal, and your changing brain and hormones amplify these feelings. Anxiety isn't something to be ashamed of. It's just your mind's way of trying to keep you safe.

The Importance of Coping: Dealing with these emotions is like learning to ride a bike. It might feel wobbly at first, but with practice, you'll get the hang of it. Why is this crucial? Because it's about taking care of your mental and emotional well-being. Just like you'd treat a sprained ankle or a cold, you should tend to your emotional health.

Building Resilience: Coping with anxiety and sadness helps build resilience—the ability to bounce back from adversity. Facing and overcoming difficult emotions, will make you more robust, more adaptable, and better equipped to handle whatever challenges life throws your way.

Seeking Support: Remember, you don't have to go through this alone. There's no shame in asking for help when you need it. Talk to people you trust—a friend, family member, teacher, counselor, or life coach. They can be your guides as you navigate this emotional roller coaster.

Self-Care: Self-care is your secret weapon against the ups and downs. Do things that make you feel good, whether it's reading a book, taking a long bath, pursuing a hobby, or spending time with loved ones. Taking care of your physical health, eating well and getting enough sleep, also has a big impact on your emotional well-being.

Looking Forward: Remember, your emotional roller coasters won't last forever. As you grow older, your wilder mood swings will stabilize, and you'll become more adept at managing them.

So, embrace your changing emotions as part of your unique journey. They're a reminder that you're growing, evolving, and becoming the incredible person you're meant to be.

I am resilient, and I can overcome
sadness, depression, and loneliness.

**I AM WORTHY OF LOVE AND SUPPORT,
EVEN WHEN I FEEL ALONE.**

I am taking one step at a time
towards healing and happiness.

I am in control of my thoughts and emotions.

I am allowed to seek help and support when I need it.

I am choosing to focus on the positive aspects of my life.

**I am nurturing my mind, body, and soul
with self-care and self-love.**

I am learning and growing from my experiences
with sadness, depression, and loneliness.

I am finding moments of joy and gratitude even in difficult times.

I am surrounded by people who care about me,
even if I can't always see it.

I AM FINDING STRENGTH IN MY VULNERABILITY.

I am allowing myself to grieve and heal at my own pace.

I am opening my heart
to the possibility of love and happiness.

I am choosing hope over despair.

**I am focusing on the present moment
and letting go of the past.**

I am a beautiful and valuable person,
no matter what I'm going through.

**Your success and happiness lie in you.
Resolve to keep happy,
and your joy and you shall form
an invincible host against difficulties.**

—Helen Keller
American author and lecturer

**Perseverance is failing 19 times
and succeeding on the 20th.**

—Julie Andrews
British actress and singer

**The most difficult thing is the decision to act.
The rest is merely tenacity.**

—Amelia Earhart
American aviator

Additional Advice

Set Small Goals: Break big challenges into smaller, manageable bits. Achieving them will boost your confidence step by step. Celebrate your victories, no matter how small they may seem.

Practice: Remember that nobody becomes an expert overnight. Whether it's learning a new skill, playing an instrument, or excelling in a subject, practice is essential. Mistakes are part of the learning process, so don't be afraid to make them.

Embrace Your Interests: Pursue activities and hobbies that genuinely interest you. When you engage in activities you're passionate about, you naturally become more confident. Whether it's art, sports, writing, math, or science, follow your passions.

Cultivate Positive Role Models: Surround yourself with people who inspire and uplift you. They can be real persons or historic figures you might learn about from reading or watching a video. Many successful people had to overcome daunting challenges, and they can be examples for you. Because they achieved great things through hard work and determination, they can motivate you to believe in yourself.

Face Your Fears: It's okay to feel scared sometimes. Again, break them down and face them one step at a time.

As you conquer them, your confidence will grow. Start with something small and gradually work your way up.

Learn from Setbacks: Instead of seeing failures as a negative thing, view them as opportunities to learn and grow. Understand that everyone encounters setbacks, and they don't define your abilities or worth.

Remain Upbeat: Surround yourself with positive people and things. Avoid negative influences that bring you down. Seek out friends and activities that make you feel good about yourself. John Maxwell, a motivational speaker, wrote a wonderful book called *Failing Forward*. A good habit to acquire.

Self-Care: Take care of your physical and mental well-being. Eat healthily, exercise, get enough sleep, and practice relaxation techniques like deep breathing or meditation. A healthy body and mind will go along way to boost your confidence.

Afterword

I hope this book has filled your heart with the confidence and determination to embrace your authentic self. I've walked the same path you're on, knowing what it's like to grapple with self-doubt, face bullying, and feel like you don't quite fit in. Growing up, I didn't have the support I needed, which made it challenging to believe in myself. I struggled with self-worth and self-esteem, enduring hurtful names and teasing from my peers. Back then, concepts like "affirmations" were foreign to me, especially in my household.

It took me a long journey to transform my mindset and truly understand that I am more than enough just as I am. I've written this book to offer you the wisdom and tools I wish I had when I was your age. Affirmations are a powerful force for change. Remember, it takes 29 days to form a new habit, and amidst the noise of social media dictating how you should look and act, always know this: YOU are more than enough just as you are.

Never let anyone dim your light or hinder your dreams. The strength within you is boundless, and your thoughts can shape your reality. In the midst of darkness, always seek the light, hold your boundaries, and choose kindness. Goodness prevails, always. Keep shining!

**There are only two ways to live your life.
One is as though nothing is a miracle
The other is as though everything is a miracle.**

—Albert Einstein

Acknowledgment

I am blessed and humbled to share this book with the world, and it is with the utmost gratitude that I recognize several, incredible individuals who have played pivotal roles in its creation. Their unwavering support and contributions have made this journey possible.

To my beautiful daughter, Ryleigh, and my wonderful son, Hunter, whose presence in my life is a constant source of inspiration and motivation. Your love and encouragement drive me to be the best version of myself every day.

To my beloved 'Mamma Linda' for being the catalyst that ignited my passion for writing. Your belief in me and your encouragement to share my voice with the world are the main reasons this book exists.

To the talented Matthew James Carmoega for his incredible work in illustrating the cover of my book. Your creativity has brought my words to life, and I am profoundly grateful for your artistic contributions.

To Bardolf & Company for believing in my work and for making the publishing process a reality. Your support has been invaluable.

And to Chris Angermann, my dedicated editor. Your exceptional efforts, guidance, and expertise have been instrumental in shaping this book into its final form.

Thank you all, from the bottom of my heart for your unwavering support and belief in me.

Dawne Christine is a professional motivational speaker and certified Mindset & Belief Systems coach, with over eight years of experience. Her journey, both personal and professional, allows her to intimately understand the struggles and tumultuous challenges many of her clients face.

Dawne is passionate about igniting the spark of inspiration within each person, encouraging them to evolve into the finest version of themselves.

In addressing the challenging and often daunting hurdles that hinder personal growth, Dawne aims to provide individuals with the tools and guidance required to break free from constraints, allowing them to experience a brighter, more fulfilled existence.

In addition to her coaching work, Dawne hosts the Podcast *Purposeful Wisdom* on YouTube.

To book Dawne for a speaking event, email her at:
dawnechristine@gmail.com
For a 30-minute, complimentary consultation, go to:
www.dawnechristine.com

www.ingramcontent.com/pod-product-compliance
Lightning Source LLC
Chambersburg PA
CBHW031218090426
42736CB00009B/963